NATIONAL
GEOGRAPHIC

Meet the Johnson Family

Jan Pritchett

Meet the Johnson family.

Anna

Dad

Sam

Mom

4

The Johnson family needs
a home to live in.

a home

The Johnson family needs food and water to keep them strong.

a home

food and water

The Johnson family needs clothes to keep them warm.

a home

food and water

clothes

The Johnson family needs
each other to get things done.

a home

food and
water

clothes

each other

These are all the things the Johnson family needs.

a home

clothes

food and water

each other